I0814606

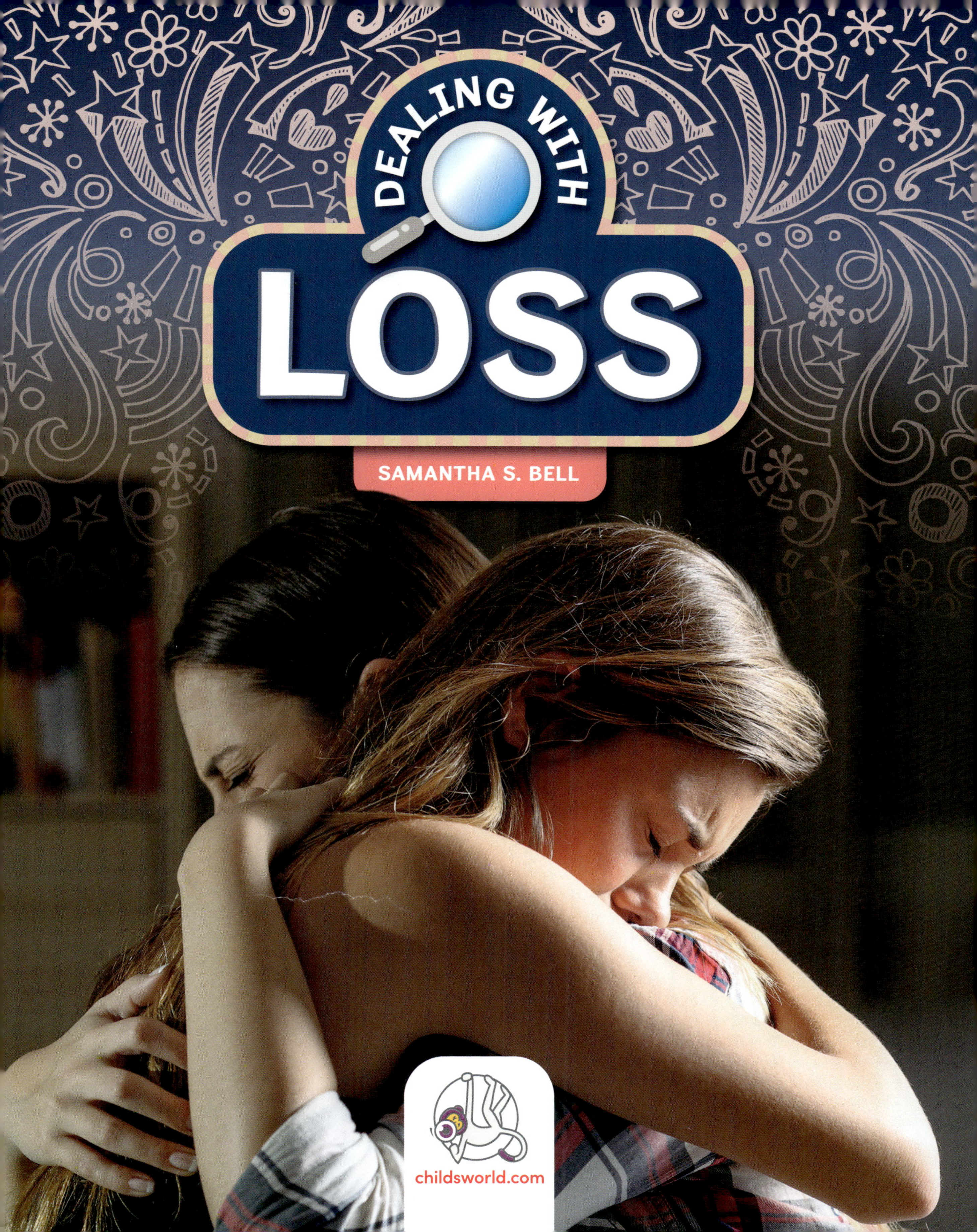
DEALING WITH
LOSS
SAMANTHA S. BELL
childsworld.com

Published by The Child's World®
800-599-READ • www.childsworld.com

Photography Credits
Photographs ©: Antonio Guillem/iStockphoto, cover, 1; iStockphoto, 5, 11, 12–13, 15, 18, 20, 22; Ground Picture/Shutterstock Images, 6–7; Shutterstock Images, 9, 17

ISBN Information
9781503885394 (Reinforced Library Binding)
9781503885615 (Portable Document Format)
9781503886254 (Online Multi-user eBook)
9781503886896 (Electronic Publication)

LCCN 2023937454

Printed in the United States of America

Samantha S. Bell lives in the foothills of the Blue Ridge Mountains with her family and too many cats. She has written more than 150 nonfiction books for kids in kindergarten through high school.

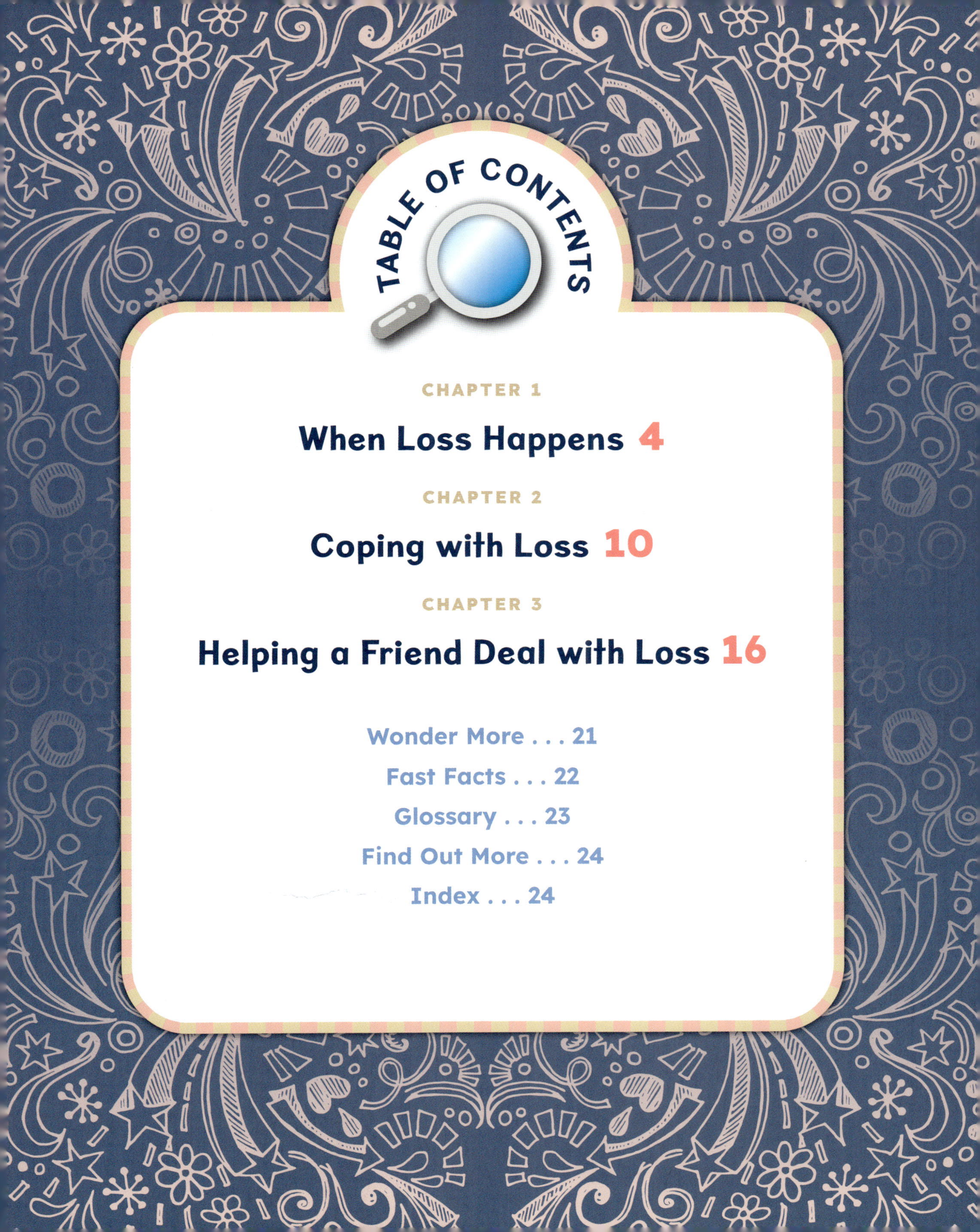

TABLE OF CONTENTS

When Loss Happens

Sometimes people lose someone or something important to them. This is called loss. People experience loss when a loved one dies. The loved one may be a family member, such as a grandparent, parent, or **sibling**. Or the loved one may be a neighbor, teacher, or friend. The loved one may not even be a person. People experience loss when a pet dies. For many people, pets provide company and friendship. It can be difficult when they pass away.

Whether the loss is sudden or expected, losing a loved one can be hard to deal with.

Grief can be caused by a move, a death, or not being able to see someone anymore.

When people experience loss, they may feel grief. Grief is a deep sadness. People may feel other **emotions** when they experience loss, too. They may be angry, afraid, or confused. They may feel lonely. They may also feel guilty. They may think they should have done more to care for their loved one. There is no right or wrong way to feel.

Grief can affect people in different ways. People who experience the same loss may have different reactions. For example, when a loved one dies, some people may cry. Others may feel angry. Some people may have a hard time paying attention. Or they may feel tired. Others might not be able to sleep, or may have nightmares when they do.

Some people may be worried or afraid about what will happen next. All of these reactions are normal parts of grief.

Feelings of grief can come and go. Some days, a person may feel very sad about the loss. Other days, a person may feel better. But then the feelings of sadness may come back again. Sometimes birthdays and holidays can bring up the sad feelings. It may hurt that a loved one is not there to celebrate the special day. It is OK to miss loved ones and feel sad.

Grief can bring up a lot of difficult feelings. It can take a long time to work through them. But the person will eventually begin to feel better.

Loss Makes Me Feel . . .

Sad

Guilty

Scared

Angry

Worried

Numb

Confused

Distracted

Tired

Loss can bring up many different feelings. All of these emotions are normal responses to losing someone or something a person loved.

Coping with Loss

People may want to get through grief quickly. But experiencing the feelings that come with grief is part of healing. Healing does not mean that people forget the person or pet they lost. Instead, people remember them with love.

One way to deal with grief is to share stories or memories about the lost loved one. Looking through photographs of the loved one can help, too. It can remind the person of happy times they spent together.

Some people make art to help them express their feelings and cope with grief.

Some people make photo albums to remember lost loved ones.

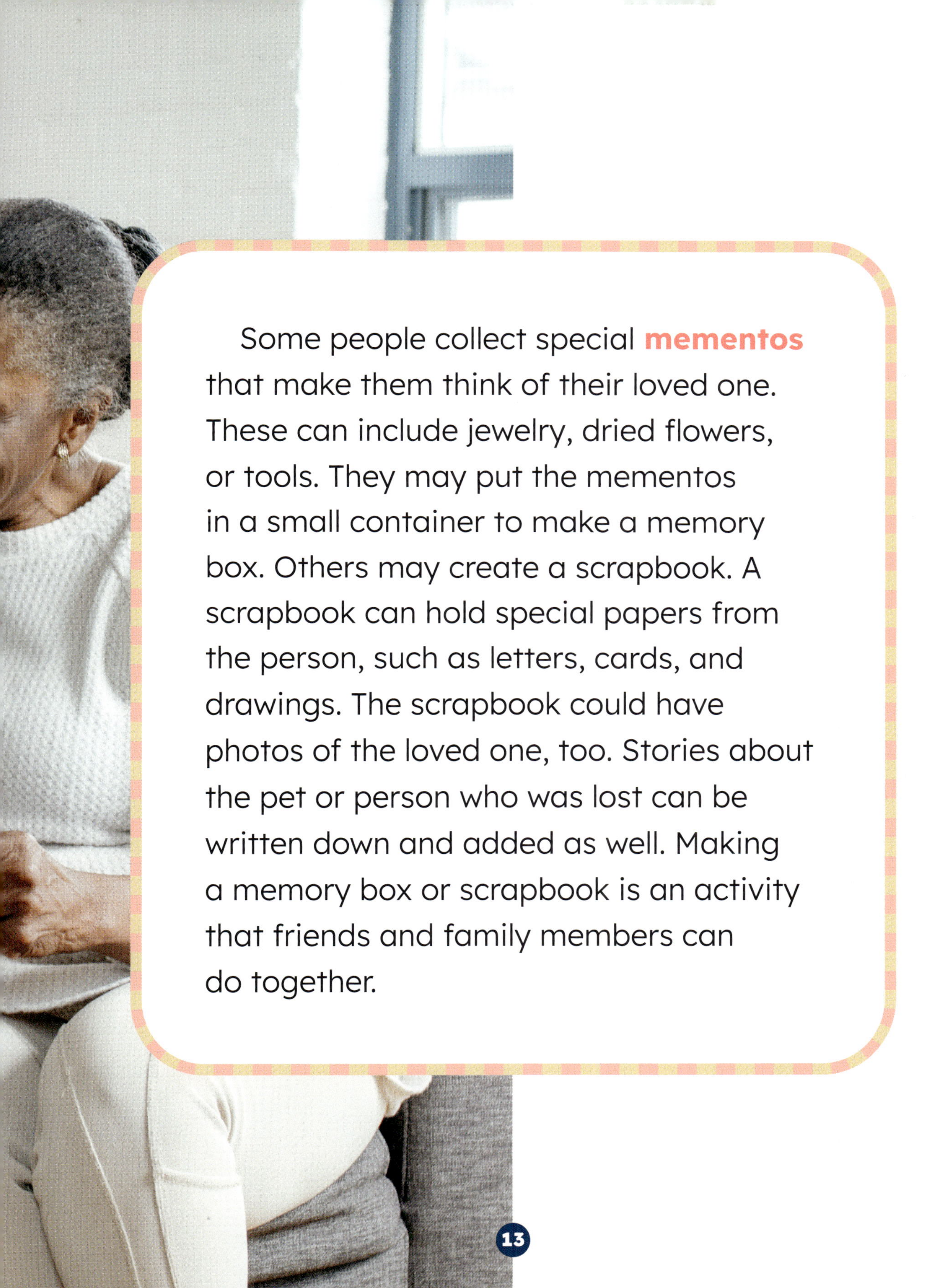

Some people collect special **mementos** that make them think of their loved one. These can include jewelry, dried flowers, or tools. They may put the mementos in a small container to make a memory box. Others may create a scrapbook. A scrapbook can hold special papers from the person, such as letters, cards, and drawings. The scrapbook could have photos of the loved one, too. Stories about the pet or person who was lost can be written down and added as well. Making a memory box or scrapbook is an activity that friends and family members can do together.

Writing is another way some people deal with grief. People who lost a loved one can write about their feelings in a journal. They can write a letter to the person or pet who died. They can tell the loved one everything they cannot say in person.

Sometimes feelings of grief are too strong to work through alone. When this happens, people can talk with someone else about how they feel. This could be a friend, a parent, or a teacher. Talking to a **counselor** can help, too. People can also join a **support group**. This can help them meet with other people who are also dealing with loss.

Being with friends can help grieving people feel better.

Sometimes doing a fun activity can make people feel better. This may be cooking, drawing, playing a game, or going somewhere. Exercise and other physical activities can help people feel better, too.

There are many ways people can work through their feelings. Everyone deals with grief differently. People need to find what works best for them.

Helping a Friend Deal with Loss

It can be hard to help a friend who has lost someone special. People may want to fix the situation for their friend. But grief is a process people must go through.

There are different ways people can **comfort** a friend. Listening is one of the most important things they can do. They can ask how the friend is feeling.

Dealing with a loss brings out many kinds of emotions. The friend may be sad.

It's important to check on friends when they're sad.

Just Be There

Many people feel like they have to say something to help their friend feel better. But many times, just sitting quietly with a grieving friend can be very helpful. Being present shows grieving friends that they do not have to deal with their sadness alone.

Some people send care packages or flowers to grieving friends.

The friend may say some things that are surprising. People should try to listen without judging what their friend says.

People can help comfort their friend in other ways, too. They can send a card. They can make their own or buy one at the store. They can write a kind note inside. People can also reach out to their friend with a phone call or a letter. Small actions like these can make a grieving friend feel less alone. It can be comforting to know that people are there.

After a friend experiences loss, the friend might have trouble paying attention in school. Helping a friend with homework or a school project is another way to show that someone cares.

Friends support each other through hard times.

Doing activities together can also comfort a grieving friend. People can choose activities the friend enjoys. This can help take the friend's mind off the loss for a little while.

Losing a special person or pet can be very hard. It is important for people to take time to work through their feelings. Then they can move forward and begin to feel better.

Wonder More

Wondering about New Information

How much did you know about dealing with loss before reading this book? What new information did you learn? Write down three new facts that this book taught you. Was the new information surprising? Why or why not?

Wondering How It Matters

Have you lost a person or pet close to you? If so, how does the information in this book relate to your life? If not, imagine how other kids who have lost someone may feel. What impact might this information have on their lives?

Wondering Why

Grief often comes with many difficult feelings. Sometimes people struggle to work through the feelings on their own. Why do you think it is important for grieving people to ask for help?

Ways to Keep Wondering

Dealing with a loss is a complex topic. After reading this book, what questions do you have about dealing with loss? What can you do to learn more about grief and how to handle it?

Fast Facts

- People experience loss when they lose someone or something they love.
- Grief is a deep sadness that can be caused by loss.
- Grief can cause many different emotions, such as sadness, anger, fear, confusion, and guilt.
- Everyone experiences grief differently.
- It takes time to get through grief.
- There are many ways to cope with grief, including sharing memories, collecting mementos, and talking about one's feelings.
- One of the best ways to comfort a grieving friend is to listen.

Glossary

comfort (KUM-furt) To comfort means to help someone feel better. A phone call or letter can comfort someone who is grieving.

counselor (KOWN-suh-lur) A counselor is a person who helps people work through strong feelings. Talking to a counselor after losing a loved one can be very helpful.

emotions (ee-MOH-shuns) Emotions are feelings, such as sadness, fear, and joy. Grief can cause people to feel many different emotions.

mementos (muh-MEN-tohs) Mementos are objects that remind someone of a person or event. Mementos may remind people of lost loved ones.

sibling (SIB-ling) A sibling is someone who one shares parents with. Losing a sibling can be very hard.

support group (suh-PORT GROOP) A support group is a gathering of people facing similar issues who come together to help each other. Joining a support group can be a good way to deal with grief.

Find Out More

In the Library

Allen, Vanessa Green. *Me and My Feelings: A Kids' Guide to Understanding and Expressing Themselves.* Emeryville, CA: Rockridge Press, 2019.

Bell, Samantha S. *Dealing with a Move.* Parker, CO: The Child's World, 2024.

Lindeen, Mary. *Feeling Sad.* Chicago, IL: Norwood House Press, 2022.

On the Web

Visit our website for links about dealing with loss:
childsworld.com/links

Note to Parents, Caregivers, Teachers, and Librarians: We routinely verify our Web links to make sure they are safe and active sites. So encourage your readers to check them out!

Index